AF531559

INSPIRING THOUGHTS
OF
SONIA GANDHI

ABOUT THE AUTHORS

Anil Dutta Mishra

Dr. Anil Dutta Mishra is a well-known Gandhian Scholar and Activist. Author of a number of books, presently he is working on "Gandhi and Women".

Email: anilduttamishra@gmail.com

Praveen Mishara

Praveen Mishara is a TV journalist, presently working with national news channel based in Delhi.

Email: praveenprabhat1@gmail.com

INSPIRING THOUGHTS
OF
SONIA GANDHI

Anil Dutta Mishra
Praveen Mishara

CONCEPT PUBLISHING COMPANY PVT. LDT.
NEW DELHI-110 059

ISBN-13: 978-81-8069-715-9

First Published 2010

Published and Printed by

Concept Publishing Company Pvt. Ltd.

Regd. Office:

A/15-16, Commercial Block, Mohan Garden
New Delhi-110059 (India)
Phones : 25351460, 25351794,
Fax : 091-11-25357109
Email : publishing@conceptpub.com,
Website: www.conceptpub.com

Editorial Office:

H-13, Bali Nagar, New Delhi-110 015, India.

Cataloging in Publication Data--*Courtesy:* D.K. Agencies (P) Ltd. <docinfo@dkagencies.com>

Gandhi, Sonia, 1946-

Inspiring thoughts of Sonia Gandhi/ [compiled by] Anil Dutta Mishra, Praveen Mishara.
p. cm.
ISBN 9788180697159

1. Gandhi, Sonia, 1946- --Quotations, maxims, etc. 2. India--Politics and government-1977--Quotations, maxims, etc. I. Mishra, Anil Dutta, 1965- II. Mishara, Praveen. III. Title.

DDC 954.05 22

PREFACE

Indian history is replete with examples of people who sacrificed everything to uphold a cause dear to them. Lord Rama chose to live in forest rather than be the ruler of Ayodhya in course of his duty to obey his parents; and Bharat, the step brother of Rama, refused to become the king of Ayodhya and occupy the throne that Rama would have occupied, because it was unethical for Bharat to usurp the rights and privileges of his elder brother. In more recent times, Mahatma Gandhi steadfastly discarded every comfort and luxury and lived like a hermit for he felt that he had no moral right to live comfortably so long as India was under the British rule and even one individual remained poor. The sacrifices that many freedom fighters made under the inspiring leadership of the Mahatma and their adherence to the values and the commitment to the cause that the Mahatma symbolized by his conduct were unprecedented indeed.

Since independence, examples of men and women of India making immense sacrifices for the causes they considered dear, have not been lacking. Smt. Indira Gandhi, the First woman Prime Minister of India, braved the dangers inherent to the steps she took to maintain the unity of the country. She sacrificed herself so that India remains united. Rajiv Gandhi, Indira's elder son, and later, Prime Minister himself, also gave his life for the national cause. Sonia Gandhi, Rajiv's wife, could have become the Prime Minister of India but she preferred to stay away. What one admires in Sonia Gandhi is her transformation from an Italian to an Indian personality. Today, she symbolizes India and Indian culture in thought, words and action. Her persona reflects the true Indian ethos.

When she took the charge as the President of the Indian National Congress (INC), the party was in disarray. She rebuilt the party brick by brick, meticulously negotiating the sharp edges of the process of reorganisation, step by step so as to ensure the party is back to the center stage of Indian politics today. As chairperson of the United Progressive Alliance (UPA), she has been able to ensure a stable government at the center and has steered the country clear through many ups and down. When the National Democratic Alliance (NDA) lost the Parliamentary elections in 2004, the UPA headed by Sonia Gandhi took charge of the country. All expected that she would take over as the next Prime Minister of India. She however, declined and preferred to contribute to and guide the future of the country from outside. Paradoxical as it may sound, she is the centre of gravity of power but keeps herself away from power. By her political maturity and conduct, she has silenced those who had been accusing her of prosecuting the pursuit of power by perpetuating family rule.

Sonia Gandhi exemplifies harmony between west and east. Born and brought up in Italy, she has adopted the Indian culture in true sprit. She speaks Hindi and has come to represent Indian womanhood better than many Indian women. One gets highly impressed by her speeches, and more so when seen in the context of her life and living ever since she landed in India as the life companion of Late Rajiv Gandhi who ushered the country in a new era of economic, technological and socio-political developments in India.

This book is on and about Sonia Gandhi. It is, however, not a biography. It is a collection of her speeches delivered from time to time in India and abroad that reflect her multi-facetted personality and thinking. As they go through the book, the readers can themselves assess what Sonia Gandhi is and what the future has to offer through her. The book is published with the sole objective of carrying Sonia Gandhi's message to people at large, especially the youth. It would remind the other leaders of the party that unless they emulate the examples set by her, they probably would not be able to connect to the people that they seek to serve.

We are grateful to all those who directly or indirectly helped us in the compilation of this work; it has been such a demanding task.

March 15, 2010
Rajghat, New Delhi

Anil Dutta Mishra
Praveen Mishara

PRINCIPAL EVENTS IN THE LIFE OF SONIA GANDHI

Edvige Antonia Albina Maino, since known as Sonia Gandhi, was born on December 9, 1946, in Lusiana village in Orbassano, a town near Turin, Italy.

Her father Stefano was in construction business and mother Paolo, took care of the family. Sonia has three sisters.

She was raised in a traditional Roman Catholic household and studied in a Catholic School.

At the age of eighteen, in 1964, she went to study English at the Bell Educational Trust's Language School, Cambridge, England.

She had occasion to meet Rajiv Gandhi, who was enrolled in Trinity College under the University of Cambridge, in 1965, at a Greek restaurant.

Sonia and Rajiv Gandhi married in 1968, following which she moved into the house of her mother-in-law Smt Indira Gandhi, the then Prime Minister.

Rajiv Gandhi left Cambridge, to pursue his passion for flying and went on to became a commercial pilot. As a pilot, he worked for the Indian Airlines.

Sonia has two children, Rahul Gandhi, born in 1970 and Priyanka Gandhi, born in 1971.

Rajiv entered politics in 1982 after the death of his younger brother Sanjay Gandhi in a plane crash on 23 June, 1980.

In 1981 Rajiv ran successfully for Parliament and took over the seat vacated by his brother. He served as the representative from the Amethi Parliamentary constituency in Uttar Pradesh.

Sonia adopted Indian citizenship in 1983.

In 1984 the Gandhi family, and indeed the entire nation, was shaken to its core when Indira Gandhi was assassinated by two of her own guards. It was in those moments of disequilibrium and chaos that Rajiv Gandhi was sworn in as the Prime Minister.

Sonia became an art historian and worked with a team of dedicated experts at the National Gallery of Modern Art in New Delhi, to restore Indian landscapes. Simultaneously, she also collected and edited the correspondence that had been between Indira Gandhi and her father, Jawaharlal Nehru, which were eventually published in the late 1980s and early 1990s.

Consequent to the election to the Lok Sabha in 1984, Rajiv was sworn in the Prime Minister. In 1989, he was voted out of office.

Rajiv Gandhi, was assassinated on May 21, 1991.

When Rajiv was assassinated, Sonia was seen by many as the natural heir and she was offered the leadership of the Congress Party. She however, rejected the offer.

In 1992 Sonia Gandhi published a book called Rajiv, which offered an intimately heither to unknown glimpses into the life she shared with her husband. In 1994 she went into greater details when she published Rajiv's World.

Meanwhile, in 1993, she visited Rajiv's former constituency in Amethi, Uttar Pradesh, and was greeted and admired by the cheering crowds. She subsequently travelled throughout the country on behalf of trusts and committees devoted to Indian public life.

She joined the Congress Party as a primary member in the Calcutta Plenary Session in 1997 and became party leader in 1998.

She contested and won Lok Sabha election from Bellary, Karnataka and Amethi, Uttar Pradesh in 1999.

She was elected the Leader of the Opposition of the 13th Lok Sabha in 1999.

On May 18, 2004, a day before the scheduled swearing in of the Government, she addressed a meeting of Congress workers and declined to become the Prime Minister.

On 28th May 2005, Smt. Sonia Gandhi was elected as President of the Indian National Congress by overwhelming support from across the country.

She holds the record of having served as Congress President for more than 10 years consecutively.

On 23 March 2006, Sonia Gandhi announced her resignation from the Lok Sabha and also as Chairperson of the National Advisory Council.

She was re-elected from her constituency, Rae Bareilly, in May 2006, by a huge margin of over 400,000 votes.

She addressed the United Nations on 2 October 2007, Mahatma Gandhi's birth anniversary which is observed as the International day of non-violence after passage of a UN resolution on 15 July 2007.

Sonia Gandhi was named the third most powerful woman in the world by Forbes magazine in the year 2004 and was ranked 6th in 2007. She was also named among the Time 100 most influential people in the world for the years 2007 and 2008.

She transformed into and adopted Indian culture in true sprit. She is Indian in real sense of the term. Not only in terms of constume, conduct, language and etiquettes, she has become a transponder of the Indian thought process, values and commitments and indeed the very Indianness. She speaks Hindi better than many other. She represents Indian womanhood par cxcellence. She had travelled the long route of head to heart and has left behind the footprints of thoughtfulness, dedication and focus on the service to the nation, for others to follow.

CONTENTS

ALIENATION

If any section feels alienated, it is incumbent upon us to deal with it most sensitivily.

[CWC Meeting, September 13, 2008]

ANGER

I believe anger and hatred blind us.

[March 7, 2009]

ASSET

The Congress Party's greatest asset is the ability to reinvigorate, modify and adapt itself to suit changing times.

[Pachmarhi Camp, September 14 , 1998]

ATTITUDE

A defeatist attitude does not help.

[February, 2009]

BALANCE

Balance is the essence of whatever needs to be done for economic growth.

[February, 2009]

BALANCE INITIATIVES

There is a need of:
Balance between public sector and private sector.
Balance between the modern and the traditional.
Balance between the urban and the rural.
Balance between the global and the local.

[February, 2009]

BASIC NEEDS

The basic needs of citizens should be fulfilled.

[Dhanbad, Bihar]

BATTLE

We are winning the battle of ideas and eventually if we act unitedly and vigorously, we will win the full support of our people.

[Pachmarhi Camp, September 14, 1998]

We adopt a fighting position where it may appear that we have a difficult battle.

[February, 2009]

BIRTH

No one is big or small by birth.

[Annual Conference of Sanitary Workers Congress, New Delhi, May 25, 2002]

BUSINESS

Successful business is about investing for the future. To build an India, in my husband Rajiv Gandhi's words, "strong, independent, self-reliant and in the front rank of the nations of the world", it is imperative that we invest together in purposeful education and training of our youth.

[The Special Plenary Session of the CII Annual Meeting, New Delhi, April 28, 1998]

CHILDREN

Every citizen of the country should get equal respect and protection; he should get share in development.

[Ramlila Ground, New Delhi, March 9, 2008]

The future of the country depends on what our children become. It is our social obligation to give them good education.

[Ramlila Ground, New Delhi, March 9, 2008]

CIVIL SOCIETY

It is not only government who are responsible for the uplift of the poor, but also the afflicted and the marginalized. Civil society too has an important role to play.

[The function organised to confer the Indira Gandhi Prize for Peace, Disarmament and Development awarded to Bill & Milindo Gate Foundation]

COALITION

The commitment to provide a strong and stable government dedicated to promoting social harmony and peace unites all of us in the coalition. The commitment to provide a firm resolute government devoted to the welfare of the kisans and khet mazdoors, youth and women and of weaker sections of society unites us all in the coalition. The commitment to provide a purposeful, effective government focused on accelerating employment, growth and investment unites all of us in the coalition.

[New Delhi, May 15, 2004]

COMMITMENT

The question we must ask ourselves is whether we have, in any way diluted our commitment to fight against communal forces. It would perhaps be tempting to say we have not. However, there is a general perception that we have at times compromised with our basic commitment to the secular ideal that forms the bedrock of our society.

[Pachmarhi Camp, September 14, 1998]

COMMON MAN

One who is attached to a common man is never weak.

[UPCC Convention, Kanpur, March 21, 2008]

COMMUNAL

Communal rhetoric and violence is not only anti constitutional, it also targets communities who have for centuries lived in India and contributed to its composite culture.

[Letters to Congress persons C.S.: Vol. XI: No. 2, 2000]

CONDUCT

We must remember that programmes, plans and preparations for election always go on in a political party. The party should remain alert about its doctrines, programmes and conduct.

[Pachmarhi Camp, September 14, 1998]

CONGRESS APPROACH

The Congress approach is founded on six basic principles.

First, sustained economic growth of 7 to 8% per year covering agriculture, industry and services in a balanced manner is a prerequisite for abolishing poverty and generating jobs.

Second, credible empowerment strategies and social safety nets are essential to ensure that the growth process facilitates a sustained and effective attack on poverty.

Third, for our economy to be strong and competitive, we must make full use of modern science and technology and of opportunities offered by the global system of trade, investment and finance.

Fourth, a fundamental reorientation of the nature and scope of public expenditure is necessary for fulfilling our social objectives relating to primary education and public health.

Fifth, effectiveness of public investment must be judged not just in terms of outlays but more importantly in terms of tangible outcomes.

Sixth, the administrative, legal and financial empowerment of local bodies, panchayats and nagarpalikas is an absolute must for ensuring that programmes of social development and poverty eradication have the desired impact.

[Special Plenary Session of the CII Annual Meeting, New Delhi, April 28, 1998]

CONGRESS GOVERNMENT

The Congress is the only party whose governments have done justice to all sections of the society and to all regions.

[April 2008]

CONGRESS PARTY

We should always be aware of the fact that the Congress is not only an organization, but is a movement. The movement is for some principle, for a point of view, for an ideal.

[UPCC Convention, Kanpur, March 21, 2008]

Congress is a party of all class of people. Congress does not differentiate between any class, caste or community. We want an atmosphere of unity and harmony. But it becomes our duty to help the poor and the weak.

[Kissan Rally, Ujjain, June 20, 2008]

The Congress Party is the party of the people.

[March 2009]

Congress is a symbol of social harmony and stability.

[March 2009]

The Congress party is a great national institution and we all take pride in being part of it. We have to lay stress on how we can bring an awakening into this great organisation. This is our commitment.

[Pachmarhi Camp, September 14, 1998]

CONGRESS PARTY CAMP

I would like Congress Party camps to be organised regularly at the national and other levels. We have so much in our lives today, but little scope for looking back; do serious thinking and self-introspection. We need all those three things.

[Pachmarhi Camp, September 14, 1998]

CONGRESS POLICY

The Congress's economic policy has not been wedded to any doctrine but has been anchored in a vision. A vision of an India free from poverty, illiteracy and malnutrition, an India with the resilience to feed itself, an India participating self-confidently in the global economy from a position of strength and an India where the fruits of growth are enjoyed by all sections of society and all regions of the country. Our economic policy is not based on any dogma nor is it founded on any magic mantra.

Our economic policy is pragmatic, our social philosophy all-inclusive and our political ideology one that integrates a strong Centre, strong states and strong panchayats and municipal bodies all drawing strength and sustenance from each other.

[Overseas Friends of Indian Congress, June 25, 2001]

CONGRESS VISION

In his centenary speech, Rajiv Gandhi etched the outlines of the programme he had in mind: "*The power to shape their own lives must lie with the people.... Vibrant village panchayats must discuss, deliberate and decide the choices to be made.*" He called this the "challenge to the Congress cadres". "*It is up to us, the workers of this great organization,*" he said: "*to spread in every village and every hamlet of India, to mobilize the people, to guide them, to stand by their side when they are denied their due...*" To this rejuvenate the Congress, Rajiv Gandhi emphasized two key issues. One, the role of ideology, policies and programmes in the everyday life of the Party. He said: "*The ideology of the Congress has acquired the status of an heirloom, to be polished and brought out on special occasions. It must be a living force to animate the Congress workers in their day-to-day activity. Our ideology of nationalism, secularism, democracy and socialism is the only relevant ideology for our great country.*" And the instrument for carrying the Congress policies to the people had, of course, to be the humble Congress worker. But the genuine Congress worker remains unheeded and unrecognised. He is not only the last to be heard but also the least heard. I see it as my primary task as Congress President to restore to the Congress the vision of the Congress centenary - Power to the People through the panchayats; and Power to the Congress worker through democracy within the Party.

[AICC Meeting, New Delhi, April 6, 1998]

CONSTITUTION

India's Constitution ranks among the foremost in the world. It represents the aspiration of our freedom-fighters and people of the nation. It is a symbol of true democracy and social justice.

[Bharat Krishak Samaj farmers session, Talkatora Stadium, New Delhi, April 17, 2000]

COUNTRY'S NEED

What our country needs most in a politics that unites, not divides: a politics that is based on service to the people and not based on narrow self-interest.

[Public Meeting at Nellore, A.P., July 17, 2008]

CRIMINALISATION OF POLITICS

Kidnapping, abduction and ransom were once the problem of the super-rich. Now, the ordinary citizen is being held hostage to the nexus between the underworld and business, the underworld and the trades union movement, the underworld and the entertainment industry, the underworld and politics. Democracy is being jeopardised by the criminalisation of politics and the politicisation of crime. In some areas there is a deplorable nexus between politics and crime. It is, therefore, most important that the MRCC took this initiative in calling together such a distinguished group of lawyers, jurists, intellectuals and concerned members of the public to deliberate on what has gone so wrong and how we are to restore safety to the citizen and ethics to our public life. The two are closely inter-related.

Unless criminals are actually intimidated by what Shakespeare called "The awful majesty of the law", not only will they be a law unto themselves, they will impose *jungle raj* on *lok raj*.

[Mumbai Regional Congress Committee, March 6, 1999]

DEMOCRACY

Democracy, including the strengthening of the Parliamentary system and also the promotion of the third tier of governance through the Panchayats and Nagarpalikas, as enshrined in the Constitution.

[Pachmarhi Declaration, September 6, 1998]

DEMOCRATIC MEANS

All the problems can be solved and there is no issue which cannot be resolved through democratic means and principles. This is my belief.

[Wanpoh, J&K, October 29, 2009]

DEMOCRATIC ROUTE

People talking of separatism must draw lessons from past and take the democratic route. Route to prosperity goes through peace and democracy.

[February, 2009]

DETERMINATION

Let us face the coming challenge with boldness, confidence and determination to win.

[February, 2009]

DISABILITY

Employing the disabled is not an act of charity. These 6 crore Indians notwithstanding their disability, constitute a valuable, talented and constructive segment of society.

Mobilising and integrating them into the employment mainstream will dramatically contribute to the growth and modernisation of the economy as a whole. Disability is no longer a welfare or charity issue. It is a development issue, an economic issue, and above all a basic human issue.

[Seminar on Employment for People with Disabilities, Calcutta, March 27, 1999]

DISARMAMENT

Ever since independence, disarmament has been at the core of India's foreign and security policy. We have always regarded nuclear and other weapons of mass destruction as a menace to human civilization and to the security of the world as a whole. We have therefore steadfastly sought the removal of this menace through the universal elimination of nuclear arms. We consider this an achievable goal, not in some dim or distant future but in a foreseeable span of time of fifteen or twenty years.

The only real moral of these developments is that in the human family of a world driven by technology and globalization, there cannot be two standards of security – one for the nuclear weapon powers and another for the rest. As my husband (Rajiv Gandhi) said in an address in 1988 —

"We must ensure that the emerging order addresses itself to the concerns, the development and future of a vast segment of the international community. and that it is not a task which can be left to a small Directorate of Powers, however strong or influential they might be".

In my view there is only one way of arresting these recent trends — sincere adherence to the goal of total

nuclear disarmament and the immediate initiation of a universally agreed, phased programme of steps for the achievement of that goal in a given period of time. I believe it is time now for a review and serious consideration of Rajiv Gandhi's "Action Plan" for a nuclear weapon-free and non-violent world.

[Speech at inauguration of the Rajiv Gandhi Chair for Peace and Disarmament, JNU, New Delhi, November 14, 1998]

DIVERSITY

Diversity has defined Indian civilisation for almost 5000 years. But as we stand on the threshold of the sixth millennia of our existence, this diversity threatens to divide us. The basic characteristic of our civilisation has been one of tolerance, accommodation, assimilation and give-and-take. While other multi-ethnic societies faded away, India has been a living example of not just Unity in diversity but also a shining embodiment of Unity through Diversity.

[Kuwait, August 29, 1998]

We have always rejected the fascistic notion of one nation, one culture, one people. We believe that India is one nation, with plural cultures, diverse peoples. Diversity has deified us for centuries.

[Pachmarhi Camp, September 14, 1998]

DREAM

I want to say that we have one dream, our target is one. Our dreams are not only for ourselves but also for our families, children and our society. I am dreaming of such a society where there is no female-foeticide, where no daughter will lose her life for dowry, where no child is left uneducated. We will together fulfill this dream.

[New Delhi, March 8, 2008]

DUTY OF THE CONGRESS WORKERS

All our political energies seem to be concentrated on elections. In between lethargy overtakes us. We must resist this. Indiscipline and indifferent performance should have no place in our Party. We must be in constant touch with our constituents. For Party workers, this means living and moving among the people. For our parliamentary and legislative representatives, it means spending a significant part of every month travelling to every corner of their respective constituencies. And our emphasis should not only be on elections but also on pressing social, economic and political issues of the day.

[AICC Meeting, New Delhi, April 6, 1998]

ECONOMIC GROWTH

If economic growth is to benefit everybody, our politics also has to be truly representative of our society and give voice to all. Panchayati Raj, which Rajivji revived in such a powerful manner, is a vital instrument of all inclusive governance.

[National Convention of BCC and DCC Presidents, Delhi, February 8, 2009]

ECONOMIC POLICY

We must constantly reinterpret our economic philosophy in the light of changing circumstances, emerging challenges and the experience we gain while implementing policies. Our economic policy will have to be multi-dimensional to meet the needs of our people at various levels. No one dogma, no one formula will cater to the diverse needs of the economy and of our society.

[Pachmarhi Camp, September 14, 1998]

ECONOMIC REFORMS

The burden and pain caused by the changes necessitated by reforms must not and cannot be allowed to fall on the shoulders of the poor or the deprived only. The burden that they carry — we all know — is much too heavy already and in the last year, it is they who have suffered the most.

[Motion of Thanks to the President in the Lok Sabha]

EDUCATION

Ultimately, education is not a financial issue but one of political will. Education, specifically primary education, must come on the agenda of political parties, legislatures, trade unions, social action groups, community and religious organisations and on the agenda of all institutions of civil society. Political parties have been preoccupied with promising equality of result. What should preoccupy us is the need to ensure equality of opportunity.

Education is beyond politics. There can hardly be any political differences over the need to spread primary education particularly among girls and female literacy particularly among the dalits, the adivasis and the minorities.

[CII Annual Meeting, New Delhi, April 28, 1998]

EFFICIENCY

Efficiency and productivity in all economic activities is a prerequisite for meeting social goals. The pattern of public expenditure must undergo a fundamental reorientation at both the Centre and in the states to enable us to invest more in poverty alleviation and social development programmes.

[Pachmarhi Camp, September 14, 1998]

ELECTION

Elections are a historic opportunity to demonstrate that we have learnt from experience and that we will function cohesively, setting personal ambitions aside for the larger good of the party to which we are all privileged to belong.

[C.S.: Vol. XI: No. February 6, 2009]

We should stay united and work together with understanding. We have to be united and offensive in our campaign. We should just not sit satisfied that anti-incumbency factor and the people will get fed-up and vote for us in our hope of getting elected in election – going states. No such things happen in the elections now a days.

[CWC, September 13, 2008]

ELECTRICITY

In the present lifestyle work comes to a halt without electricity.

[Bikaner, September 8, 2008]

Without power there can be no progress.

[Devil (Tonk), September 8, 2008]

EMPLOYMENT

The Congress's top priority has always been employment-intensive growth. Growth without creation of jobs is socially unacceptable. At the same time, mere increase in jobs without growth and productivity is simply not sustainable.

[Special Plenary Session of the CII Annual Meeting, Vigyan Bhawan, New Delhi, April 28, 1998]

EMPOWERMENT OF WOMEN

We want to involve women in every step so that they can themselves face the problem, they should develop self-confidence and become independent.

[Siri Fort, New Delhi, March 8, 2008]

ENEMY

We are often our own worst enemies.

[Congress Parliamentary Party, February 25, 2009]

ENEMY OF PEOPLE

Once again some people with the help of terrorism are trying to create terror by killing innocent people. They want to disturb our unity and harmony. Such people are the enemy of our society and our country.

[Panipat, October 2, 2008]

ENTREPRENEURSHIP

......theme today revolves around the three Es – the economy, employment and education. Let me underline a fourth E: entrepreneurship. I believe Indian entrepreneurs are second to none. Some of our domestic entrepreneurs have already become global players.

Some of our non-resident entrepreneurs have become international giants. It is this drive, vision and spirit that will sustain India in the years to come. There is a new generation of Indian entrepreneurs-professionally skilled, self-confident, aggressive, customer-focussed and not afraid to take on competition. They deserve every support and encouragement.

[CII Annual Meeting,
New Delhi, April 28, 1998]

EQUITY

While it is true to say that in the nineties economics, finance and trade occupy centre space, it must at the same time be remembered that the economy exists to serve the people and to meet their basic needs. We cannot lose sight of wider ethical issues and concerns such as equity and the environment. Gandhiji emphasised this time and again. Nehru's concept of mixed economy has stood the test of time even though the nature of the mix must vary with the changing needs of the time. However, State intervention can be effective only if politics recaptures the high moral ground and its role as a purposeful instrument of social change.

[AICC Meeting, New Delhi, April 6, 1998]

EXPECTATION

We must be realistic in our expectations.

[AICC Meeting, New Delhi, April 6, 1998]

FARMER

All of us know that the farmer is provider of food. Now, if the farmer is disappointed, if his back is breaking due to the burden of debt, if there is no progress in agriculture then the country cannot develop and country cannot become strong.

[New Delhi, March 9, 2008]

I came into politics with a purpose to contribute all that I could to the welfare of our people, to the strengthening of our party and to preserving the secular heritage and tradition of our land.

[C.S, VOX, No. 7, March 2008]

The life of everyone in the country depends on the hardwork of the farmer.

[Devil (Tonk), September 8, 2008]

The life of the society goes on due to the toil of the farmers. The farmer has been called provider of food grains but I want to call the farmer provider of life.

[Kissan Rally, Sangli, Maharashtra, March 17, 2008]

Our farmers are the backbone of our country.

[National Convention of BCC and DCC President, February 8, 2009, Ramlila Ground, Delhi]

FIGHT

In our eyes all the people of India are equal even if they belongs to different religions or caste. Our fight is against the politics of differences; our fight is against social injustice. Our fight is against atrocities.

[Delhi, March 6, 2000]

FIRM VIEW

My resolve will in fact be all the more firm, to fight for our principles, for our vision, and for our ideals.

[Congress Parliamentary Party Meeting, Delhi]

FOREIGN POLICY

Foreign policy is not something of concern only to diplomats. It affects each and every one of us. It is fundamental to our security, to our standing in the world, to our very sovereignty. It impacts on the economy, on our exports, on our ability to mobilize foreign investment for development. The very financial position of the government is affected by foreign policy.

[Pachmarhi Camp, September 14, 1998]

FREEDOM MOVEMENT

The Indian freedom movement was dedicated to a purpose and not to a doctrine and the purpose was to eliminate as far as possible, in a pluralistic society, inequalities and caste bias.

[Pachmarhi Camp, September 14, 1998]

GENDER EMPOWERMENT

Gender empowerment is no longer a distant dream but a palpable reality. It is the progress we as women have made that must encourage and spur us to higher levels of achievement. Complete gender equality, nothing less, must be our over-riding goal. There must be neither compromise nor complacency. The struggle has been joined. It must be brought to full fruition.

[March 8, 1999]

GOVERNMENT

A government's true test is by its work and recognized through its concern for the people.

[Bikaner, Rajasthan, September 8, 2008]

A government should work under law and limitations and should have respect for the people. Where there is no law and order there remains nothing and there is just a rule of the jungle.

[Amreli, Gujarat, December 8, 2007]

GRASSROOTS

Our leadership must in fact emerge from the grassroots. It must reflect the aspirations of the grassroots. It must be sensitive to the demands of the grassroots.

[AICC Meeting, New Delhi,
April 6, 1998]

GREAT DREAM

The founders of the Congress party and the leaders who were at its helm in the last 50 years all shared a great dream. Above all they wanted:

- To build an India free from poverty, ignorance and disease.
- To build a dynamic economy which would provide work for our youth; food, clothing and homes for our millions.
- To build a compassionate society where health and literacy would be available to all.
- To build a self-confident India, holding its head high in the ranks of the world's nations.
- And to build a just, equitable and harmonious society in which the great diversity of our country would be celebrated and all our rich and varied cultures would co-exist. I believe this is the India we still want for ourselves and our children.

[Bangalore, January 15, 1998]

GROUPISM

The Congress Party can be strengthened and rejuvenated only when the dedicated and committed Congress workers get access to the organization and are not sidelined because of groupism or factionalism.

[Speeches on becoming Congress President, April, 1998]

GROWTH

Growth for us has never been only about per capita income figures. It has always been a means to an end.

[CS: Vol. XI, No. 3, November, 2008]

Growth alone cannot be sufficient. Reforms involve a reliance on market-based solution, but disadvantaged groups may not be able to tap these opportunities because they do not have resources, education or even information. Therefore, as Professor Amartya Sen has argued, it is necessary to step up government spending in areas like primary education and rural health. But can this be done without cutting down on other government subsides that do not necessarily benefit only the poor? And what impact will this have on inflation?

[Jawahar Bhawan, New Delhi, December 6, 1998]

HARMONY

India's identity is that all religions and communities co-exist in harmony.

[C.S.: Vol. XI: No. 6, February, 2009]

HARMONY AND BROTHERHOOD

No society can progress without the spirit of harmony and brotherhood.

[25 May, 2002]

HERITAGE

Our task is nothing less than saving, preserving, nourishing and passing on to coming generations the genius of the heritage of this ancient land and the unique saga of our freedom movement.

[CPP General Body Meeting, February 24, 2008]

INDEPENDENCE DAY

India's Independence Day must remind our workers, of the principles of non-violence and communal harmony that Congress has always championed.

[CS: Vol. X, No. 12, August, 2008]

INDIA

For our young people who dream of India as a country capable of fulfilling a responsible international role in the future, it is imperative to guard against ideologies that malign the ethos of our pluralist culture.

[C.S.: Vol. XI, No. 1, January, 2009]

INDIA OF MY DREAMS

In the years since Rajiv Gandhi left us, I had chosen to remain a private person and life away from the political arena. My grief and loss have been deeply personal. But a time has come when I feel compelled to put aside my own inclinations and step forward. The tradition of duty before personal considerations has been the deepest conviction of the family to which I belong.

I became part of India thirty years ago when I entered Indira Gandhi's home as her elder son's bride. It was through my husband's love and compassion for his people that my heart opened to their pain and suffering. It was by living so close to Indira Gandhi and Rajiv Gandhi, by experiencing first hand their dedication and passionate love for India, and by witnessing their example and sacrifice, that I imbibed my unwavering and absolute devotion to our country and her people.

Like all of, I have been pained at the growing violence we see around us, the communal divide spurred by religious fundamentalism and cynical politics which seek to separate people from one another by barriers of religion, caste and region. I am anguished when I witness the exploitation of the poor and disadvantaged, especially women and children who are the most vulnerable members of our society.

I share the frustration of every Indian with the deterioration in the quality of public life and the loss of those values which made our county great and our people proud. The founders of the Congress Party and the leaders who have shaped its destiny over the last 50 years all shared a great dream. Above all they wanted:

- To build an India free from poverty, ignorance and disease.
- To build a self reliant economy which would provide work for our youth; food, clothing and home for our millions.
- To build a just, equitable and harmonious society in which the great diversity of our country would be celebrated and all the rich and varied cultures of our people would co-exist.
- And to build a strong self-confident India, holding its head in the ranks of the world's nations.

This is the India we still want for ourselves and our children.

[Hyderabad, January 16, 1998]

INDIAN CIVILISATION

Indian civilization and culture give tremendous importance to unity and brotherhood. The village and farmers living in the villages are the greatest example of cooperation and coexistence. This is the culture of our nation.

[Bharat Krishak Samaj Farmers Session,
Delhi, April 17, 2000]

INDIA IN THE 21st CENTURY

As Rajiv Gandhi said:

"As we build today
so will be the tomorrow.
Together we will build
for an India
of the 21st century.
Together we will transform.
What needs transformation.
Together we will face
challenges and obstacles
to progress.
Together we will create
an India that is strong, wise
and great -
a flame of peace and tolerance."

[AICC Meeting, New Delhi, April 6, 1998]

Our objective is not to win elections alone. In life, there is both success and failure. Victory ultimately goes to those who stand up for the Truth, who are ready to sacrifice their all for their principles. I want that Congress which is prepared to do this task. Let those who wish to go with me do so knowing this full well, and let those with the slightest reservations about this go their own way. We have neither fear nor concern. We are not lusting for office. We are not among those who run after power. Our task is the service of the nation, the completion of the work and the realization of the dreams of the great souls who have gone before us. No one and nothing can tear us from this goal.

What is the meaning of their questioning my patriotism? Mother India took me to her bosom thirty-one years ago, the very day I came here as Indiraji's daughter-in-law. Not only has this land borne witness to my life, every second of my life has mingled with this land. It was here that I married, here that I became a mother, here before your eyes that I was widowed. The greatest daughter of this country, Indiraji, breathed her last in my arms. Each drop of blood in my being cries out that this is my land. This is where I belong, this is my country.

It is not I who will answer those who question my nationality, it is the people of this country who will give them a befitting reply. As regards the post of Prime Minister, as is customary when the occasion arises, this will be decided by Congress Parliamentary Party.

The Congress Party has always made the struggles of the people its own. We have always sought to maintain democracy, ensure social equality, and promote justice for all. The history of our Party is replete with this endeavour. Our struggle is to keep the flame of these principles burning. It is to us that the people of this country look their eyes brimming with hope. It is to us that they turn in the hope of a better life, of a better world, in the hope that we will keep the promise of their yearning for a brighter future.

My husband Rajiv Gandhi, who forsook his personal inclination to work in the public domain, focussed the energies of our people with a sense of mission towards achieving greatness in the 21st century.

Our commitment from the beginning has been to help the poorest of the poor, to relieve the pain of the tormented in communal strife, to lift the weakest and less-abled, to give voice to the underprivileged, the oppressed, the untended. This is still our primary concern. We believe that the Indian woman, so long unable by circumstance to contribute fully in our national life, should in the new century find her rightful place as equal partner in every sphere of human endeavour. I particularly look to my young compatriots, our new generation of Indians whose expectations and ambitions encompass the world. I assure them of our full support, as they become the cutting edge of India in the new Millenium.

We are the world's largest democratic party, which seeks to play a decisive part in the future fortunes of the world's largest democracy. Our task is great and this greatness shall invest our every thought and effort, abjuring the trivial and the irrelevant ones.

Ours is not a battle merely for votes or for public office, as they like to portray it. It is certainly not a referendum on personalities, to which they wish to confine it. It is a battle for the India of our dreams, for the future of our children and our children's children. I invite every Congress worker and supporter in India and abroad to join us in this historic battle. This is a battle for the minds of all right thinking Indians, by which I mean all Indians, to rise above regionalism and casteism, to rise above gender and economic disparities, to rise above the divisive squabbles of petty politics, to rise above the destructive mind-set of apathy and despair.

To all my fellow-Indians, I call out to join us in building a new, strong, united and resurgent India.

[Talkatora Stadium, New Delhi, 2000]

INQUIRY

An administrative inquiry into a possible lapse by the administration has no credibility.

[Meeting of the General Body of the CPP on August 22.]

KHADI

Khadi was the thread that united the people of different communities, classes and regions throughout the country into the fabric of resistance to foreign rule.

Gandhiji wrote: "Swaraj has no meaning, for the millions unless they are given the means to employ their enforced idleness". And a quarter century later, in one of his articles on the subject in the Harijan of 29th June 1947, Gandhiji said "The centre of swadeshi lies in Khadi".

Khadi is soul of India

[CPP General Body Meeting, February 24, 2008]

LEGACY

On the basis of past legacy we have to form our future.

[C.S.: Vol. XI: No. 6, February 2009]

We, as Indians, are heirs to a legacy of humanism, tolerance and equality, which alone can protect our noble heritage, ensure progress and our fair name in the world.

[January 30, 1999]

LOOK FORWARD

Some of us often see only the dark side. I have neither the 'all is well' and so 'sit back hand in hand' attitude nor do I see despair and defeat all around.

We must harbour neither of these in our minds. Neither complacence nor pessimism will behove us. We have to look forward to the future. We have to learn from the past, not remain stuck with it.

[Pachmarhi Camp, September 14, 1998]

MAHATMA GANDHI

It is not the relevance of Mahatma Gandhi that is in question today... it is whether we have the courage to emulate his preaching's and what he lived and died for.

[U.N. General Assembly, October 2, 2007]

MARTYRDOM

There is no greater tribute we can pay to Mahatma Gandhi, and all he did so passionately stood for, than to rededicate ourselves to fighting the forces which created the atmosphere of hate in which he was martyred.

[Martyrdom Day of Mahatma Gandhi,
January 30, 1999]

MESSAGE FOR CONGRESS WORKERS

Resolve to restore the Congress to its original values of service and sacrifice.

Resolve to restore to the Congress its ethical and moral foundation.

Resolve to continue relentlessly in building a new Congress, a Congress that once again represents the hopes and aspirations of a growing number of our people, a Congress that embodies an India marching confidently forward providing prosperity, dignity and pride to all its citizens.

[Pachmarhi Camp, September 14, 1998]

MISERY

Travelling across India extensively, I have witnessed the utter misery of the poor in rural areas. Recent events have shown that while the farmer must get a reasonable price for his output, inefficiencies of the distribution system can result in unaffordable prices which especially hurt the poor. Yet, public expenditure on agriculture has to increase if we are to increase the levels of productivity. The form and content of that public expenditure has to be improved to take out the inefficiency from the system.

[Jawahar Bhawan, New Delhi, December 6, 1998]

MOVE AHEAD

Let us move ahead united, with a sense of purpose and discipline.

[C.S.: Vol. XI: No. 6, February, 2009]

NATION

A nation that starts fooling around with its Constitution, shakes the very foundation of its existence.

[Bharat Krishak Samaj Farmers Session,
New Delhi, April 17, 2000]

NATIONAL PARTY

Nation needs a national party like Congress.

[C.S.: Vol. XI: No. 6, February, 2009]

Our Congress Party is the only truly national party with a vibrant presence throughout the country.

[C.S.: Vol. XI: No. 6, February, 2009]

NEW GENERATION

The future of a country is moulded by the new generation.

[Kissan Rally, Guwahati, June 13, 2008]

NON-ALIGNMENT

Non-alignment, as relevant as even in the post-Cold War era to the conservation of our sovereignty, and our relentless struggle to end what Shri Rajiv Gandhi called the "quest for dominance" which regrettably continues to characterise international relations.

[Pachmarhi Declaration, September 6, 1998]

OBLIGATION

It is basic constitutional and ideological obligation for us to ensure that each and every citizen is able to lead a life of security and dignity.

[CWC, September 13, 2008]

OPPOSITION

It is not the business of the Opposition to ensure the survival of a government that has lost its majority.

[PCC Presidents & CLP Leaders' Meeting, May 6, 1999]

ORGANIZATION

The organization is an army. We are all its soldiers. You have given me the status as the chief of this army. Therefore, I hope that whatever decision the party takes, whatever the policies the party frames, whatever programmes the party makes, it is the duty of a soldier to implement them. We are all bound by this rule.

[UPCC Convention, Kanpur, March 31, 2008]

No success can be achieved in any field without a strong organization.

[UPCC Convention, Kanpur, March 21, 2008]

PANCHAYATI RAJ

Panchayati Raj is the basis of our democracy. During the independence struggle, Mahatma Gandhi had given the slogan of gram-swaraj. This simply meant that free India's democratic system should not merely be manifested at a superficial level, it should arise from the grassroots. Our is a nation of villages. Our democracy cannot be deemed to be fully successful until the people living in far-flung corners of the country begin to feel that the power to determine their future and take decisions about local progress lie in their hands. All the freedom-fighters, nation-builders and members of the Constituent Assembly wholly agreed with this perception of Mahatma Gandhi. After independence, we have progressed in various fields of life but some shortcomings have crept into the realm of Panchayati Raj. As a result of the politics of power and personnel considerations, it came to be increasingly neglected. In several states, elections to panchayats ceased to be held on time. Elected bodies came to be dissolved without rhyme or reason. The importance of the government increased, panchayats and municipalities were rendered helpless in the face of the administrative machinery. The voice of the villages and ordinary citizens was suppressed.

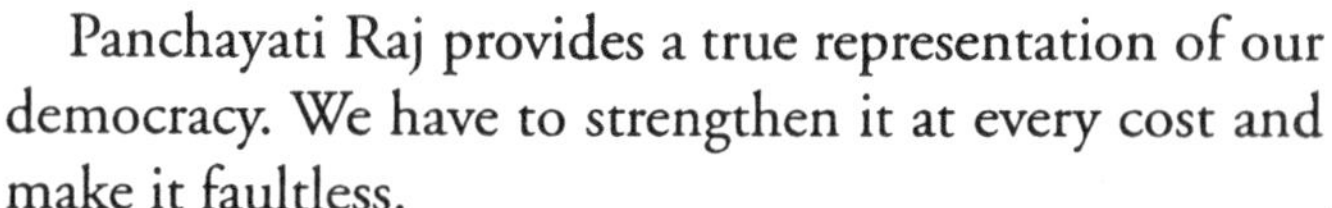

Panchayati Raj provides a true representation of our democracy. We have to strengthen it at every cost and make it faultless.

The Congress party respects everyone in society. However, our attention is focused on those who have been left behind on the road to progress. It was from this perspective that Gandhiji spoke of upliftment of the poorest of the poor. That is why I want to exhort you to give importance not to the post to which you have been elected but to the service of the people. Act in accordance with the belief that you have not been given a position, but responsibility.

I want to convey this very message to ministers, members of the legislative assemblies and Parliament. Without this attitude the love of the people cannot be won. To earn the regard of the people and keep it intact is the greatest test.

[Panchayati Raj Conference, Bhopal]

PARTY

We must remember that the party comes above all and its ideology and goals must guide our workers to work unitedly for our victory.

Letter to Congress persons [C.S.: Vol. XI, No. 1, January, 2009]

Our task is to give the people of India an organization that stands for them, that fights for their rights and is anchored to the principles on which our nationhood is founded. We must shun what is expedient and stand by what is right. That is what Gandhiji taught us. This simple truth wrested for our Independence from the mightiest military power then known to history.

[AICC Meeting, New Delhi, April 6, 1998]

PATRONAGE

Patronage and quota system must not have a role to play.

[C.S.: Vol. XI: No. 6, February, 2009]

Rajivji realised that in a country such as ours, so complex, so large and varied the people had to be empowered to govern themselves.

[Kuwait, August 29, 1998]

Rajiv Gandhi asked; "*What has become of our great organization? Instead of a party that fired the imagination of the masses throughout the length and breadth of India, we have shrunk, losing touch with the masses.*" It was by firing the imagination of our people that Gandhiji won us our freedom. It was by firing the imagination of the people that Panditji and Indiraji built an India of which the nation was proud. And it was through what he called "*a politics of service to the poor*" that my husband sought to ignite the imagination of the people.

[AICC Meeting, New Delhi, April 6, 1998]

POLITICAL BEHAVIOUR

We must honour the traditions of our Parliament and gain the confidence of the people by setting high standards of moral and political behaviour. Having said that I must stress that our members will be expected to severely and relentlessly oppose any attempt at diluting policies and programmes central to the well-being of our people.

[AICC Meeting, New Delhi, April 6, 1998]

POLITICAL OPPONENT

We must aggressively counter the negative propaganda of our political opponents.

[C.S.: Vol. XI: No. 6, February, 2009]

We have to be cautious of our political opponents, but at the same time, we also must have an eye on black sheep amongst us.

[C.S.: Vol. XI: No. 6, February, 2009]

POLITICAL WORK

Our party has been serving the people since the days of Mahatma Gandhi. We should remember what Gandhiji said- "political work can be done only by adhering to ideals and morality."

[Pachmarhi Camp, September 14, 1998]

POLITICS

We need more good people, more educated people, more professional people, more skilled people in our politics. Politics is not just about elections and tickets and ministerships. It is about making a difference to the lives of millions of the disadvantaged, the deprived and the discriminated. It is about having a higher vision of service and sacrifice. It is about being an instrument of social change and transformation. Let me also admit that while politics is important, we must not neglect the task of strengthening the institutions of civil society.

[Kuwait, August 29, 1998]

The use of religion for political purpose, often blatantly encouraged by established parties, goes against the basic principles of our Constitution. It stands opposed to India's own tradition of cultural plurality. The problems of poverty, illiteracy and discrimination affect members of every community and need to be address at the national level by all political parties. No one must be allowed to play politics.

The Congress Party's greatest asset has been the ability

to reinvigorate, modify and adopt itself to suit changing time. The Congress enjoys great goodwill amongst people of all sections. It is upto us to tap the vast reservoir of support by the force of our thoughts, words and deeds.

[CS: Vol. X, No. 12, August, 2008]

POLITICS OF OPPOSITION

The politics of our opposition is narrow-mindedness, discrimination and selfishness. Their politics is the politics of sowing the seed of discord. They are not bothered about if there is disintegration in the society due to religion, caste and region or due to any reason, they are only worried about to capture power at any cost. The congress cannot compromise with such politics. We have learned this thing from our ancestors and nation-builders.

[Kissan Rally, Sangli, Maharahstra, March 17, 2008]

POVERTY

The bulk of India's poor live in rural areas and are dependent on agriculture for their livelihood. Even urban poverty is often a spillover of rural poverty. So, if poverty is going to be eliminated in India, Agricultural reforms are essential.

[Jawahar Bhawan, New Delhi, December 6, 1998]

POWER

The people would be the ultimate power. People's power is stronger than the despot governments.

[C.S.: Vol. XI: No. 6, February, 2009]

Power in itself has never attracted me, nor has position been my goal.

[Congress Parliamentary Party meeting, Delhi]

The Congress has always believed that ultimate purpose of power is to wipe out the tears from the eyes of the last man.

[February, 2009]

PRINCIPLES

I must abide by the principles, which have guided me all along.

[Congress Parliamentary Party Meeting, Delhi]

PROGRESS

Our country cannot make progress unless development takes place in our village.

[Ahmadnagar, Maharashtra, June 19, 2008]

PUBLIC SERVICE

To do public service, there should be true feeling, determination and love in your heart for the people from every section of the society, particular from the poor and weaker sections.

[Bikaner, Rajasthan, September 8, 2008]

RAJIV GANDHI

Sriperumbudur is a place of great sadness, but it is also a place of inspiration for me. The passage of time has not made it easier to be here. My heart is filled with deep emotion. For all the years we were married, my husband was the centre of my life and existence, he was a loving and protective father to our children.

But Rajiv Gandhi was much more than a husband and father. He was a man of the masses, who put his country and his people before himself. When destiny summoned him to leave his chosen career and private life, he answered the call with complete commitment. He drew strength from the boundless love of his countrymen and women, he reached out to the poor and disadvantaged, to learn from them and to help them to the best of his ability.

Some of you may have seen him, perhaps heard him speak and felt the powerful force of hope and concern which he radiated. Millions upon millions of our countrymen and women looked up to him as a leader and a person of virtue and goodness. We knew him to be a man of courage and principle, a leader of compassion and fortitude, and a statesman of foresight and wisdom. In the chronicles of our nation's history, he will be remembered as a true and noble son of India.

In coming here I pay homage to Rajiv Gandhi and I grieve for him. My husband's sacrifice may have removed him from our midst. His voice may have been silenced. But his powerful message and what he stood for is still vibrant and alive.

Today, the India of his dreams is being increasingly threatened. In the past few years, I have shared the distress of every right thinking Indian as I have watched our country in crisis. I have been anguished and angered at the way our people are being used and misled.

Where we once had principles and values in public life, we now witness the cynical exploitation of the common man and woman by political vested interests whose only concern is to grab power at any cost. Like many of you I have been pained by the cynicism which drives so many parties and politicians to appeal in the name of religion, caste or region.

In the years since Rajiv Gandhi left us, I had chosen to remain a private person and live a life away from the political arena. My grief and loss have been deeply personal. But a time has come when I feel compelled to put aside my own inclinations and step forward. The tradition of duty before personal considerations has been the deepest conviction of the family to which I belong.

I became part of India thirty years ago when I entered Indira Gandhi's home as her eldest son's bride. It was through her heart that I grew to understand and love India. It was through my husband's love and compassion for his people that my heart too opened to their pain and suffering.

It was by living so closely to Indira Gandhi and Rajiv Gandhi, by experience first hand their dedication and passionate love for India, and by witnessing their example and sacrifice, that my devotion to our country and her people is unwavering and absolute.

We do not want our society to be broken up into fragments. We do not want our people to be separated from one another by caste or language, religion or region. We do not want our sisters and daughters brutalized, our sons and brothers killed in cold blood, no matter to which community they belong.

As a country we prize our diversity. In spite of periods of tensions and turmoil we have lived together for generations, we have lived as friends and neighbours. In moments of trial we have always stood together as one people. I believe that the Congress party is the only truly national party representing the whole country and all its people. It is the party which under Mahatma Gandhi, Jawaharlal Nehru and scores of freedom fighters from all parts of the country, so many of them from this very region, earned India her freedom.

The institutions we have, the economic growth we have achieved, our place in the world, democracy itself, these are all achievements largely of the Congress party.

Although I am conscious of its shortcomings, I am convinced that under the right and able leadership it is the only party which has the experience and capability to give India what it needs most at this time – a stable government which will work without fear or favour, for the benefit of all Indians.

The people of our country want education for our children, health care for our families, employment for our youth, social justice and economic prosperity. We want to improve our standards of living. We want homes to live in, clean water, electricity, the basic amenities every human being requires. Our women want to be empowered, and want an end to exploitation in any form. Our people want to be able to lead lives free from fear and tension, to go about daily chores in peace, without having to beg or bribe for what is rightfully due to them.

Every Indian has the right to live in dignity and self-respect. But we cannot achieve what we seek without upholdig our national traditions and values of democracy, secularism and social justice. I will work with Congress party to serve our people with hopes renewed and courage of our conviction. Let us work together to re-build a strong, just and prosperous nation.

[Sriperumbudur, January 11, 1998]

REAL ECONOMIC GROWTH

We recognise that a necessary pre-condition to solving these problems is real economic growth. This is based on fairly strong correlation between high growth rate and poverty reduction across several countries. Growth provides resources that can be used for direct anti-poverty measures. What then needs to be done to achieve high growth rates? That is where efficiency, competition and reforms become important.

[Jawahar Bhawan, New Delhi, December 6, 1998]

RELIGION

Religion is used to show the right path to those who have lost their way.

[C.S.: Vol. XI: No. 7, March, 2009]

RELIGIOUS FUNDAMENTALISM

Religious fundamentalism is alien to our culture but let us not be smug about this. Forces of religious fundamentalism of all kinds are out to destroy this tradition of tolerance and mutual accommodation.

[Pachmarhi Camp, September 14, 1998]

RESPONSIVE POLITICAL FORCE

We have a special responsibility for attracting and retaining good people into our fold. Our party must dedicate itself to cleansing public life, we must be a more responsive political force. An effective instrument of social justice. We are committed to electoral reforms to reduce the role of money and muscle power.

[Pachmarhi Camp, September 14, 1998]

REPRESENTATION

If economic growth is to benefit everybody, our politics also has to be truly representative of our society and give voice to all.

[C.S.: Vol. XI: No. 6, February, 2009]

RICH AND POOR

Today the need is to reduce the gap between the rich and the poor. The poor must get all the necessary facilities. This is not asking for benevolence rather it is your right.

[Annual Conference of Sanitary Worker Congress,
New Delhi, May 25, 2002]

RIGHT STEPS

We should not stop in our steps and keep moving ahead.

[Panipat, October 2, 2008]

ROLE OF GOVERNMENT

The role of the government at every level has to be redefined in the light of changing circumstances to make it a vehicle of economic change and social transformation. This is the essence of economic reforms. Government expenditure must add to the country's productive investment capacity and must be focused on improving the nation's physical and social infrastructure.

[Pachmarhi Camp, September 14, 1998]

ROLE OF WOMEN

Rajivji's observations on the role of women in our lives and as part of it, in a speech he delivered to a conference of chief ministers on Panchayat Raj. He said, and I quote:

"It is women who undertake much more than half the economic activities in rural India. It is women to whom are entrusted the welfare and, often, the finances of the household. It is the women of rural India who are the main repository of India's great cultural traditions, of the moral values which are fundamental to the survival and efflorescence of our civilization... Should we not begin the process of reservations for women at the lower tier in the hope that it might in due course expand upwards to the higher tiers?"

[March 8, 1999]

SACRIFICE

Our party believes in sacrifice and following in the footsteps of great people like Guru Gobind Singhji, who had not simply fought against the injustice but had also created a sense of confidence among the people. Do not fall prey to the empty promises of our opponents. The Congress is committed to the overall development of the region."

[Nanded, Maharashtra, October 7, 2009]

SCIENTIFIC TEMPER

India cannot be a modern and forward looking nation without inculcating in the people a scientific temper. The whole country too must nurture excellence in science and technology and take dynamic initiatives to apply them to benefit social and economic development. We have to mobilize our vast talents and our great pool of human resources to take our country forward keeping especially in mind the needs of the poor and the disadvantaged among our sisters and brothers.

[Bangalore, January 15, 1998]

SECULARISM

Secularism, that is the bedrock of our nationhood, draws its essence from catholicity, humanism and respect for every faith and religious denomination in the world, is consecrated in our Constitution, is the immutable commitment on which our democratic polity rests, and is enshrined in the Congress concept of secularism as defined in the past, the present and will continue into the future;

[Pachmarhi, September 6, 1998]

Rajivji was a passionate advocate of secularism, and perhaps his most comprehensive remarks on the subject were made in his intervention in a discussion in the Lok Sabha on 3 May 1989. He set out in that speech three major principles of secularism.

"First and foremost," he said, "our secularism is not anti-religious or irreligious. We have a deep and abiding appreciation of the rich vein of spirituality which runs through our culture."

"Our second great principle" he said, "is that we respect all religions equally. No religious community is

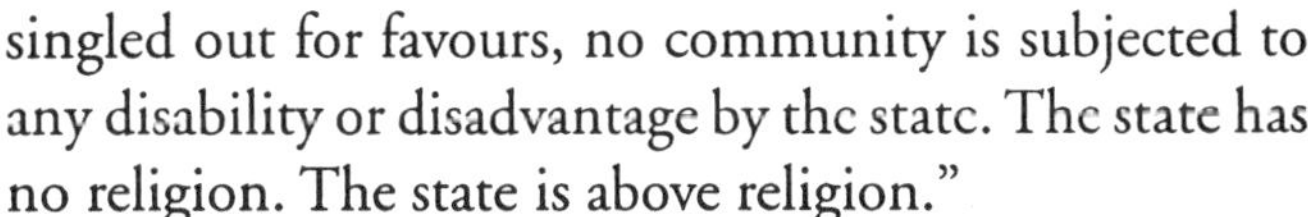

singled out for favours, no community is subjected to any disability or disadvantage by the state. The state has no religion. The state is above religion."

"The third principle" he added, "is that religion has high value but must remain in the sphere of private and personal life." And from these three principles, he drew the fundamental proposition: "Mixing religion with politics is against the traditions of our civilization, the canons of our constitution and the survival of our State."

Deliberate attempts are being made to undermine our institutions for narrow sectarian ends. The essentially inclusive nature of the Indian people and Indian nation is being threatened. Nowhere in our philosophical tradition or in our historical experience is there any justification or evidence for the politics of hatred.

Our country needs a secularism of conviction to a secularism of convenience. That conviction must be inner conviction springing from within.

We pray for a secularism born of inner moral values, a secularism nourished by passionate conviction, a secularism upheld by courageous action.

Secularism means equal respect for all religions. This is the only basis for India's unity and integrity. This was the dream of Mahatma Gandhi and Jawaharlal Nehru. This is what Indira and Rajiv Gandhi laid down their lives for. It is a complete negation of our values and heritage to convert religion into an instrument to divide. All religions and all communities have a right to their beliefs and a right to feel secure.

[Hyderabad, January 16, 1998]

SECURITY AND SAFETY

In a democracy, governed by rule of the law, each Indian has a total freedom to move within and work anywhere in the country. No one has a right to displace anyone just because he does not belong to a region. It is the responsibility of those in authority to ensure the security and safety of everyone.

[C.S., Vol. X, No. 8, April, 2008]

SOCIAL JUSTICE

Politics has certainly given new identities to disadvantaged groups and has empowered oppressed communities. But we must take the social justice movement into its next phase, into a phase that stresses basic issues of health, education, food, security, nutrition and family planning.

[Pachmarhi Camp, September 14, 1998]

As a free society, we believe in the freedom to pursue prosperity, but not at the expense of social justice.

[CS: Vol. XI, No. 3, November, 2008]

Prudence implies ensuring an economic system that imposes clear, fair rules and rewards those who play by them.

[CS: Vol. XI, No. 3, November, 2008]

SOCIALISM

Socialism, directed to the task of promoting equity and social justice, based on sustained, balanced and high economic growth, through a mixed economy allied to democratic institutions of governance.

[Pachmarhi, September 6, 1998]

SON AND DAUGHTER

The women should also understand that there is no difference between a son and daughter. There is a need to make our every off spring healthy, educated, capable and skilful.

[New Delhi, March 8, 2008]

SPINNING WHEEL

In a country such as ours, sophisticated capital intensive manufacture and information technology related industry are no substitute for employment through the spinning wheel and potters wheel..

[CPP General Body Meeting, February 24, Parliament]

SPIRIT OF INDIA

Jawaharlal Nehru said that India was not a mere geographical expression or just a historical entity but the very mind of india, its unique capacity to welcome alien influences and synthesizing the best of these influences into a coherent and composite heritage. Nowhere else has the principle of unity in diversity been raised, as it has been in India over the millennia, into a civilisational principle, the very basis of our nationhood. Take away this unshakable dedication to diversity and the very spirit of India disappears.

The Freedom Movement harnessed that civilisational principle into the practical politics of building a nation. We have succeeded in holding together this vast and diverse country, owing to several reasons. Foremost among them are the wisdom and farsightedness of our Founding Fathers and the great leaders who followed them. No less important is the fact that the people of India are by nature, secular and respect, in their hearts, all faiths.

Our people understand that our unity is safe as long as our diversity is assured. You will recall that thousands of years ago our ancient seers had proclaimed that the world is one family. Now the rest of the world is waking up to this fact.

It is, therefore, disturbing that within the country an assault has of late been mounted on these most fundamental values of nation-building. This assault takes many forms, one of which is to dacry secularism and all that Jawaharlal Nehru stood for, to malign him, and his personality and his historic contribution. But Jawaharlal Nehru's contribution is so towering that it can survive any battering by prejudiced politicians and their skewed history. But if the mind of India, particularly the young mind, is led wodn twisted paths, it could do lasting damage to the essence of our being as a nation. It is that endeavour which we must guard against. Secularism is the cause for which Jawaharlal Nehru worked with all his phenomenal energy.

Speaking at the Ram Lila grounds on Mahatma Gandhi's birth anniversary in 1951, Panditji said:

"If any man raises his hand against another in the name of religion, I shall fight him till the last breath of my life - Whether I am in government or outside."

In the name of religion, many hands are being raised today against the life and limb, and rights and property of persons of other religious persuasions. The very identity of the children of Mother India is being questioned. It is the struggle to protect and cherish our plurality, whether one is in government or outside, that constitutes the heart of our political agenda.

[November 13, 1998]

STATUS OF WOMEN

Women in India have, through history, been the victims of a cruel paradox. On the one hand, woman power is celebrated as Shakti - the source of all energy, the life force of the cosmos. Yet, in actual social practice, an oppressive dependence was encouraged as the social norm. Independence of both thought and action were frowned upon, indeed, even prohibited on pain of punishment and ostracisation. Of course, there were exceptional women. They are celebrated in myth and legend, in saga and history, in verse, in music and dance. But the very exceptionality of these women underlines the unfortunate condition of the vast majority of womanhood.

[March 8, 1999]

STRUGGLE

On the one side you have struggled for the cause of the country while on the other, you have the experience of many a struggle in your life.

[Bikaner, September 8, 2008]

Our struggle has been for secular democracy and social justice.

[Speech on the release of the AICC manifesto, March 24, 2009]

STRUGGLING FOR NEW HISTORY

The world is moving fast. India too has to move with this pace. Leaders like Gandhiji, Jawaharlal Nehru, Maulana Azad, Indiraji and Rajivji had seen such a dream that we are able to stand with pride before any nation of the world. They had seen this dream and we get inspiration from this dream. We are not worried about today, we are not worried about tomorrow but we are worried about the coming future. This way a new history is made and we are struggling for it.

[Kissan Rally, Usmanabad, Maharashra, March 17, 2008]

TERRORISM

Terrorism, in all its manifestations, can be combated only if we are united as a society, and are one as a country.

[National Convention of BCC and DCC Presidents, February 8, 2009, Delhi]

Terrorism is not and can never be a solution to any grievances and only leads to further polarization of society.

[C.S.: Vol. XI: No. 6, February 2009]

Terrorism, in all its manifestations, can be combated only if we are united as a society, and are one as a country.

[C.S.: Vol. XI: No. 6, February 2009]

Only a united and secular India can counter the menace of terrorism effectively.

[March, 2009]

TRYST WITH DESTINY

A divided India cannot survive. A fractured India cannot prosper. An India in which Indian is set against Indian cannot keep its 'tryst with destiny'. The respect for plurality and the celebrations of diversity constitute the very essence of Indian civilization.

It is the Congress party which under the leadership of Jawaharlal Nehru, Indira Gandhi and Rajiv Gandhi has brought and weaved together sections of society harmoniously. We are the only political party that has not, does not and will not practice the policies of exclusion and the politics of spreading animosities.

The Congress is a place of dignity and respect for all communities, for all religions, for all languages, for all regions that make up the kaleidoscopic mosaic of India.

[Pachmarhi Camp, September 14, 1998]

UNABLE TO FACE

People who for their selfish politics take advantage of the situation in dividing the society. They feel that success will come to them only through this path. The society which gets divided on the basis of hatred and sentiments is unable to face any big challenge.

[Panipat, October 2, 2008]

UNHOLY POLITICS

It is our foremost duty to defeat these unholy divisive politics by partisan people.

[Amreli, Gujarat, December 8, 2007]

UNITY

Nobody will benefit in raising the walls of caste or communalism. Any society progresses only due to its unity.

[Dhamangaon, Maharashtra, October 4, 2004]

History is witness that we progress when we act unitedly and we fail to progress when we fight with each other. We achieved freedom on the basis of our unity and on the strength of our unity our nation has made progress.

[Dhamanagar, Maharashtra, October 4, 2004]

The incidents which are happening in the recent past has really hurt the whole of India. The people who indulge in these type of work and belong to any religion are hardly a well wishers or friend of anyone.

[Ramlila Ground, Delhi, May 29, 2009]

The unity of our country is due to social unity. We should clearly understand that national integrity is our real strength and this is the key to our progress and development.

[Amreli, Gujarat, December 8, 2007]

There is no great strength than unity.

[Panipat, October 2, 2008]

UNITY AND INTEGRITY

We all know, we have achieved our freedom with how much difficulty. How many patriots have sacrificed their lives and lakhs of freedom-fighters by their sacrifices and renunciation had kept the flame of freedom burning. Our leaders have sacrificed their lives for the sake of our social unity and integrity.

[Panipat, Haryana, October 2, 2008]

VICTORY

The victory of the party is a victory for all of us. Victory of groups is also a victory for individuals. But it is a matter of regret that we forget this fact and deliberately neglect it. For our self-interest and ambitions we lose in elections and make the party weak.

[CWC, September 13, 2008]

Let us not revel in our victory. Let us greet it as a welcome opportunity to effect the changes that may better the lives of our brothers and sisters all over India. Let us understand the sentiment behind this mandate. Let us each acknowledge that the people of India have chosen us to represent their aspirations not our own.

[New Delhi, May 15, 2004]

WALK ALONE

I think fighting alone will give us a bit of space to build ourselves.

[C.S.: Vol. XI: No. 7, March, 2009]

WIDOWHOOD

Widowhood is both a personal tragedy and a concern for society as a whole. With family support and counseling, widowed women can be helped in their personal sorrow and bereavement. Where society comes in the obligation to equip women with the educational, economic and social strength to look after themselves and their families when calamity strikes. This is where our collective efforts assume importance.

There was a time when widows were looked upon as bringers of misfortune. They were shunned and marginalised even by their families. The worst of these practices of the past are mercifully behind us. But there are segments of our society where prejudices persist. Nor can it be said that mindsets have fundamentally changed. While widows are treated with greater respect and sympathy than was once the case, such sympathy tends to be tinged with feelings that they and their children are an additional burden that must be borne. Changing societal mindsets is our first responsibility.

In doing so, the key lies in education. I believe the nation's highest priority should be primary education. Within that priority there is a special need to focus on the education of the girl-child.

It is estimated that there are 35 million widows in the country, many not yet grown to womanhood. They need to be integrated into their extended families and society. Yet, many suffer social ostracism, which leads to exploitation in many guises. We have to raise our voices against discrimination and oppressive cultural practices. No religion is discriminatory – only practices and interpretations are discriminatory. Gandhiji stressed that women must come out of their homes and take their place in ever increasing numbers in the building of our modern nationhood. With this in view, we must encourage widows to put aside their grief and sorrow and come into the mainstream.

[National Seminar on Widows-Neglect and Social Action, February 26, 1999]

WINNING IN ELECTION

You are aware that when we win in election, it is because of our work, unity and well meaning policies. But when we lose, we do not always lose to our political opponents, but sometimes to our lack of unity and because of few blocks in the bottom of certain hearts.

[C.S.: Vol. XI: No. 6, February 2009]

WOMAN'S EMPOWERMENT

The woman empowerment is much a journey which is full of challenges and responsibility. It requires a lot of patience and determination.

[New Delhi, March 8, 2008]

Our must also be the party which gives real responsibility to women. Tokenism will not do and is, indeed, offensive, women must not find themselves shelved and marginalized into just their frontal organization.

[AICC Meeting, New Delhi, April 6, 1998]

WOMEN

Women are the strength of mankind. Their well-being is the well-being of whole families.

[National Convention of BCC and DCC Presidents, February 8, 2009, Delhi]

Women are the strength of mankind. Their well-being is the well-being of whole families.

[C.S.: Vol. XI: No. 6, February, 2009]

The single most significant achievement of the twentieth century has been the liberation of women. If we cast our mind back a hundred years we will see that so much we take for granted was then deemed inconceivable, impossible, and outrageous.

[March 8, 1999]

The development of our country and our states, will, in true sense, be through the progress of our women.

[Kissan Rally, Guwahati, June 13, 2008]

Sometimes, we forget that women are not general citizens. They are true strength of our society. They are the epicentre of our family and given birth to the future. As per Indian tradition, women are the embodiment of force.

[New Delhi, March 9, 2008]

WORKER

The basic foundation of any political party is their workers. The strength of the Congress would depend upon how strong we want to keep it. The strength of the party is directly related to the will-power, we have to keep it strong.

[CS: Vol. XI, No. 6, February, 2009]

YOUTH

Youth are the future of our party.

[February, 2009]

Our Party has to renew itself by attracting the best and the brightest of the young to join and contribute to its growth. Youth needs encouragement; youth needs opportunity; youth needs training.

Youth is idealistic. It is wary of the unsavoury. It is inspired by the moral high ground. We will spot promising young talent; we will nurture it; we will promote it. We will identify with the aspirations of the new generation and make them feel that, establishment though we are for over a century, we are conscious of their concerns and responsive to their quest for answers. Ours will be a Party which gives real responsibility to the youth.

[AICC Meeting, New Delhi, April 6, 1998]

A systematic campaign is called for to enhance the image and the standing of the Congress among special groups in society-among the youth. We must not alienate ourselves from this vast, growing and dynamic segment of our society. Our programs and policies must be such that they engage and draw the youth to our party. Their concerns must be addressed. It has now become clear that college degrees are not going to solve the problem of educated youth. What we need is education that is job-oriented and we intend to put this into effect when in office.

[Pachmarhi Camp, September 14, 1998]